The Buck Stops Here

Legal and Ethical Responsibilities for United Methodist Organizations

Mary Logan

General Counsel
General Council on Finance and Administration
of The United Methodist Church

DISCIPLESHIP RESOURCES

P.O. BOX 340003 • NASHVILLE, TN 37203-0003
www.discipleshipresources.org

Cover design by Sharon Anderson

Book design by Joey McNair

Edited by Debra D. Smith and Heidi L. Hewitt

ISBN 0-88177-306-9

Quotations identified as 1996 *Discipline* are from *The Book of Discipline of The United Methodist Church—1996*. Copyright © 1996 by The United Methodist Publishing House. Used by permission.

Scripture quotations identified as CEV are taken from the Contemporary English Version. Copyright © 1991, 1992, 1995 American Bible Society. Used by permission.

Scripture quotations, unless otherwise indicated, are from the New Revised Standard Version of the Bible, copyright © 1989 by the Division of Christian Education of the National Council of the Churches of Christ in the USA. All rights reserved. Used by permission.

DR306

Contents

Introduction

The kingdom is also like what happened when a man went away and put his three servants in charge of all he owned. The man knew what each servant could do. So he handed five thousand coins to the first servant, two thousand to the second, and one thousand to the third. Then he left the country.... Some time later the master of those servants returned. He called them in and asked what they had done with his money. The servant who had been given five thousand coins brought them in with the five thousand that he had earned.... "Wonderful!" his master replied. "You are a good and faithful servant. I left you in charge of only a little, but now I will put you in charge of much more. Come and share in my happiness!... Everyone who has something will be given more, and they will have more than enough. But everything will be taken from those who don't have anything."
(Matthew 25:14-15, 19-20a, 21, 29, Contemporary English Version)

Serving in the many available volunteer church leadership roles is a basic part of being a member of a faith community. Stewardship of our time is as important as our gifts of money. All too often, we who serve on boards and committees do not take our roles as seriously or as objectively as we should. We work hard all day at our "paid" or other unpaid jobs, taking care to make decisions that are in the best interests of the organizations we serve. What happens when we become a board member of a church organization? Sometimes we feel too busy or burdened to be truly engaged in the role. At other times, we have personal agendas that get in the way of careful objectivity. Or we think God will provide where we fail to do so. Some church organizations also have a naive tendency to think that churches are somehow immune from the scrutiny of the outside world in terms of how we conduct our church business.

These comments are certainly not intended to overlook the loyalty, dedication, and hard work of tens of thousands of volunteers who serve in these church leadership roles. Churches could not survive without us. However, we all can benefit from the occasional gentle nudging about the seriousness of our duty to the church when we serve in these positions of leadership.

This handbook is intended to be a practical guide to understanding your obligations as a member of a church board or committee. It should be mandatory reading for every volunteer who serves on a church board or finance committee. If you are one of those volunteers, it will help you understand your legal and ethical responsibilities, thus enabling your organization to more effectively carry out its mission.

Board members need to ask questions—and ask those questions as if their own personal retirement fund were at stake in the decision they are about to make. The board that goes through a careful, objective analysis of each issue presented to it, asking questions based on a thorough presentation and review of a complete set of materials about an issue, will almost always make decisions that are in the best interests of your church organization and the church overall.

Who Should Read This Handbook?

In Local Congregations
- board of trustees
- church council or administrative board
- programmatic and mission-related boards of directors (church daycare, preschool, homeless shelter, and so forth)
- finance committee
- endowment boards and committees
- executive committees of United Methodist Women and United Methodist Men

In Districts
- board of trustees
- board of church location and building

In Annual Conferences
- conference board of trustees
- council on finance and administration
- camping ministry boards

Others
- foundation boards
- officers of general boards and agencies
- directors and members of executive, finance, investment, and audit committees
- affiliated organization boards where United Methodist leaders serve by virtue of their position (bishops, district superintendents, council directors, local presidents of United Methodist Women and United Methodist Men, and so forth)

If I were to boil down the traits of a good church board member to one essential characteristic, it would be this: Tone at the top. The actions and inactions of the board set the tone at the top for how all others in the organization can and will behave. Board members serve as role models for the organization, with respect to living out our Christian values. The church is like a giant fish bowl. Those who work for and with you will observe your behavior and conduct; those who know the staff of your organizations will observe the same. What exactly will they see? What tone are you setting at the top?

Following the suggestions in this handbook will result in board credibility, fiscal integrity, and the trust and confidence of donors.

Mary Logan, General Counsel
General Council on Finance and Administration
of The United Methodist Church

Chapter One

Keys to Good
Board Governance

Awe came upon everyone, because many wonders and signs were being done by the apostles. All who believed were together and had all things in common; they would sell their possessions and goods and distribute the proceeds to all, as any had need. Day by day, as they spent much time together in the temple, they broke bread at home and ate their food with glad and generous hearts, praising God and having the goodwill of all the people. And day by day the Lord added to their number those who were being saved. (Acts 2:43-47)

Every church organization should engage in an ongoing evaluation of its own governance. A church board or committee is healthy, vibrant, and probably making all of its decisions in the best interests of the organization if it

■ continually asks: "Are we governing the organization well?";

■ engages in an ongoing evaluation of itself;

■ takes that evaluation to heart in changing unhealthy behaviors;

■ monitors the changes and holds itself accountable.

The following list of questions will help your board or committee engage in a self-evaluation. This self-evaluation can be done informally by you, as a board or committee member, by asking yourself the questions and doing some reflective thinking about each question. Or it can be done more formally as part of a board or committee meeting (or series of meetings), leadership retreat, strategic planning process, organizational meeting, or leadership training event.

✓ Are board members nominated and renominated only after thoughtful consideration and evaluation of their skills and commitment?

✓ Is the board diverse, or is it controlled by a small group or faction?

✓ Is there an effective evaluation process for the chief executive officer/senior pastor?

✓ Does the board adequately understand its role?

✓ Does the staff provide the board with complete and adequate information?

✓ Do board members adequately prepare for meetings and give the issues their utmost attention and care?

✓ Does the board make key policy decisions about the organization?

✓ How is conflict managed?

✓ Does the staff make day-to-day operational decisions?

✓ Are decisions based on the best interests of the total organization, or do special interests dominate decisions?

✓ Do all members feel that their opinions and ideas are valued, or do some feel disenfranchised?

✓ Are the board members providing real leadership in the organization?

✓ Is God at the center of the board's decision-making process?

✓ Are Christian values respected by the board at all times?

✓ What tone at the top does the board set for the entire organization?

Chapter Two

Basic Responsibilities of Serving on a Church Board

Ten bridesmaids took their lamps and went to meet the bridegroom. Five of them were foolish, and five were wise. When the foolish took their lamps, they took no oil with them; but the wise took flasks of oil with their lamps. As the bridegroom was delayed, all of them became drowsy and slept. But at midnight there was a shout, "Look! Here is the bridegroom! Come out to meet him." Then all those bridesmaids got up and trimmed their lamps. The foolish said to the wise, "Give us some of your oil, for our lamps are going out." But the wise replied, "No! there will not be enough for you and for us; you had better go to the dealers and buy some for yourselves." And while they went to buy it, the bridegroom came, and those who were ready went with him into the wedding banquet; and the door was shut. Later the other bridesmaids came also, saying, "Lord, lord, open to us." But he replied, "Truly I tell you, I do not know you." Keep awake therefore, for you know neither the day nor the hour. (Matthew 25:1b-13)

What Is a Board Member?

Serving as a member of the governing board of a church organization can be one of the most rewarding, challenging, stimulating, and difficult roles a volunteer will ever perform. It is a serious role with significant responsibilities. The governing board of a church organization is responsible for making the policy decisions for that organization, protecting its assets, and charting a course for its future. All are important and weighty concerns. While every church organization is unique, the role and responsibility of the board ultimately is the same for all church organizations. Boards and board members perform best when they stick to the basic responsibilities outlined in this handbook.

Important Resources

United Methodist organizations are required to comply with *The Book of Discipline of The United Methodist Church—1996.* This is the law of the United Methodist denomination and is published every four years following General Conference. All references in this handbook to specific provisions in the *Discipline* are based on the 1996 *Discipline*, which includes a wide variety of rules that apply to governing boards. For example, ¶ 2553 of the *Discipline* states in part: "Trustees of schools, colleges, universities, hospitals, homes,

Every church organization needs a clear mission that is lived out in ministry.

orphanages, institutes, and other institutions owned or controlled by any annual, jurisdictional, or central conference or any agency of The United Methodist Church shall be at least twenty-one years of age."

The Judicial Council is the "Supreme Court" of The United Methodist Church. Judicial Council Decisions also constitute the law of the church. These Decisions are printed in *General Minutes of the Annual Conferences of The United Methodist Church* or can be found on the Internet at http://www.umc.org/churchlibrary/judicial.

The Book of Resolutions of The United Methodist Church—1996 contains the resolutions approved by the General Conference. Once approved, these resolutions become official policy statements that guide the work and ministry of The United Methodist Church. Both the *Discipline* and the *Book of Resolutions* can be ordered from Cokesbury (800-672-1789).

Board members of United Methodist organizations need to be mindful of their obligations, and the obligations their organizations, under these various sources of United Methodist polity, policy, and law.

Basic Responsibilities

Commitment to the Organization's Mission and Ministry

Every church organization needs a clear mission that is lived out in ministry. It is the board's responsibility to be committed to that mission. This mission should be clearly articulated in a concise written statement, usually no longer than one page in length. Anyone who reads the mission statement should be able to understand what the organization does and why, as well as who is served by the organization. From time to time, the board should review the organization's mission and revise it as needed, in order to keep it updated, focused, and compelling. All organizational activities should support its mission and ministry.

Planning

Organizational planning involves setting measurable goals and objectives that translate the mission into active ministry. A basic responsibility of the board is to oversee the planning process. Depending on the size of the organization, the planning process may be initiated by staff or committees under board guidance or direction, or it may be done entirely by the board. At a minimum, the board's role will be to evaluate the strengths of the plan and to ask questions, such as the following:

✓ Does the plan support the organization's mission and ministry?
✓ Are the priorities clear?
✓ What are the financial implications of the plan?
✓ Do all of the activities in the plan support the mission and ministry of the organization?
✓ What are the costs and benefits to the organization for each program or service it offers?
✓ How can the organization more effectively fulfill its mission?
✓ What assumptions underlie the goals and objectives? Are these assumptions realistic?

✓ Is the organization adequately staffed to carry out the plan?

✓ Does the board need to conduct a self-assessment as part of the plan?

✓ Are goals clear and have benchmarks been set for measuring progress toward the goals?

✓ What are the risks to the accomplishment of the plan, and how can the risks be reduced?

Resources

Providing adequate resources for the organization to carry out its mission is a key responsibility of the board. The board models stewardship, promotes giving, and raises new funds.

Protecting Resources

A key responsibility of the board, directly related to its fiduciary role (see Chapter Three), is protecting the organization's resources effectively. This primarily includes approving the budget, reviewing financial reports, establishing internal financial controls, overseeing an audit, setting reserves, overseeing investments, formulating policies (investment, ethics, conflict of interest, travel, internal control, and so forth), insuring against risks, monitoring the budget, being aware of signs of financial distress, and the like. The board should ask questions and receive information about each of these issues on a regular and ongoing basis.

> *Having a clear mission, together with an organizational plan with measurable goals and objectives, is invaluable to the board.*

EXAMPLE

In 1994, the United Way of Santa Clara County, California, had $12.6 million in reserves and a budgeted net annual revenue of $25 million. In May 1999, the reserve was gone and the organization faced a budget deficit of $11 million, making it unable to fund its commitments. Attendance at board meetings was never one hundred percent, and some meetings had no quorum. In June 1999, the entire board resigned. What happened? The organization engaged in a well-meaning and well-planned campaign to attract large donors. The expensive campaign failed, and the board completely depleted its reserves and went into deficit spending to continue to fund the campaign over an extensive period of time. When it finally became clear to the board in 1999 that the organization was in serious financial trouble, the executive director cut staff almost in half and offered extremely generous severance packages to those who were terminated. This is an excellent example of a good organization that failed to monitor the budget, be aware of signs of financial distress, use financial controls, and provide the diligent oversight and guidance that a board must provide.

Evaluating the Organization's Performance

Having a clear mission, together with an organizational plan with measurable goals and objectives, is invaluable to the board in its ongoing role of evaluating the organization's effectiveness in carrying out its mission and ministry. The evaluation process, which can range from simple questions to surveys and focus groups, involves essentially four parts:

Constituents will feel good about giving when they trust that an organization is being managed well, fulfilling its mission, protecting the contributions, and doing the work of the church.

■ The board asks whether it is governing the organization well.

■ The board engages in an ongoing evaluation of itself. (This includes asking, "How effectively are we carrying out the organization's mission?" and evaluating and adjusting the budget to ensure that it is balanced between administration and program.)

■ The board takes that evaluation to heart in changing unhealthy behaviors and activities that do not fulfill the organization's mission. (This includes asking how the organization can or should change its policies or priorities, in order to carry out its mission more effectively in the future.)

■ The board monitors its changes and holds itself accountable.

Ensuring Legal and Ethical Integrity

All nonprofit organizations have come under increased public scrutiny in recent years, and church organizations today are feeling the same pressures for accountability that publicly held corporations have experienced for decades. Too many instances of fraud, embezzlement, and cover-ups have led to public distrust. If organizations such as the United Way of America can experience fraud of the worst kind, then so can a church organization.

It is the board's responsibility to set policies to guide the organization in a legal and ethical manner. A conflict-of-interest policy is a good start (see pages 16–18). The board is also responsible for ensuring that the organization adheres to local, state, and federal laws; develops and follows adequate personnel policies and procedures; adheres to the organization's bylaws and articles of incorporation; complies with the *Discipline;* obtains adequate legal advice before making decisions with potential legal implications; and so forth.

Image and Integrity

A board that takes its basic responsibilities seriously will go a long way toward maintaining and enhancing its image of competency and integrity with its constituents and the public at large. The board can be proud of its accomplishments and promote the organization's image when these basic responsibilities are met. Good media relations, press releases, speeches, annual reports, and a sense of open communication will enhance this image even more. Constituents will feel good about giving when they trust that an organization is being managed well, fulfilling its mission, protecting the contributions, and doing the work of the church.

Effective church organizations go beyond what is minimally necessary to maintain accountability. Why? Because its integrity is all a church organization has. A breach of trust is a powerfully difficult obstacle to overcome. Avoiding the appearance of impropriety plus caring for organizational assets are key to maintaining the trust of constituents.

EXAMPLE

William Aramony, former President and CEO of the United Way of America, was convicted of fraud (a felony) in a criminal action against him and found guilty in a civil lawsuit filed by United Way of America against him. He was required to pay $50,000 punitive damages and $232,138 in consequential damages for costs arising from the scandal. He also was ordered to return $951,250 of his salary (because a disloyal employee forfeits his right to compensation for services performed during the period of disloyalty). In the criminal case, Aramony was sentenced to seventy-eight months, keeping him in prison until age seventy-five. In its decision in the civil case, the court made the following comments:

> Defrauding the United Way is akin to an attack on motherhood or the flag. Millions of Americans have contributed to the United Way, intending to benefit the neediest members of our society. Aramony's conduct, in some small way, squandered those contributions....

Most legal proceedings against high-level executives for embezzlement do not involve outright theft of large amounts of money. Rather, they involve the improper payment by the organization of the personal expenses of the executive. In the case of William Aramony, one striking aspect of the entire matter is that most of the criminal charges of which he was convicted were based on seemingly mundane personal expenses that he charged to the United Way.

Chapter Three

Fiduciary Duty

A prince once went to a foreign country to be crowned king and then to return. But before leaving, he called in ten servants and gave each of them some money. He told them, "Use this to earn more money until I get back."… After the prince had been made king, he returned and called in his servants. He asked them how much they had earned with the money they had been given. The first servant came and said, "Sir, with the money you gave me I have earned ten times as much." "That's fine, my good servant!" the king said. "Since you have shown that you can be trusted with a small amount, you will be given ten cities to rule." The second one came and said, "Sir, with the money you gave me, I have earned five times as much." The king said, "You will be given five cities." Another servant came and said, "Sir, here is your money. I kept it safe in a handkerchief. You are a hard man, and I was afraid of you. You take what isn't yours, and you harvest crops you didn't plant." "You worthless servant!" the king told him. "You have condemned yourself by what you have just said. You knew that I am a hard man, taking what isn't mine and harvesting what I've not planted. Why didn't you put my money in the bank? On my return, I could have had the money together with interest…. Those who have something will be given more. But everything will be taken away from those who don't have anything." (Luke 19:12-13, 15-23, 26, CEV)

The Basics

Many people who give the gift of their time in The United Methodist Church serve in roles that place them in a position of fiduciary responsibility. They stand in a special relationship of trust, confidence, and responsibility toward others in the organization. Examples of roles in the church that carry a fiduciary (trustee) responsibility include: boards of trustees, administrative boards, finance committees, and foundation/endowment boards of a local church, district, or annual conference; annual conference councils on finance and administration; directors of other foundations and endowment boards; directors of general agencies; and other roles in which there is a responsibility to manage funds or other assets and direct the work of the organization.

The funds of local churches, annual conferences, and the general agencies are derived primarily from the contributions and gifts of individual donors in local churches. Such funds also may be received by other means, such as pension contributions, gifts, bequests, and profits generated by the sale of materials. Those who manage and control church funds—and assets acquired from those funds—are trustees of those asset funds, with the obligation to manage and administer those asset funds properly and to direct the work of the local church, agency, organization, or group, in accordance with the directives of the General Conference (as embodied in the *Discipline*, the *Book of Resolutions*, and elsewhere) and in compliance with secular law.

Secular law imposes two basic duties on all trustees: the duty of loyalty and the duty of care.

Duty of Loyalty

The duty of loyalty imposes two basic obligations on a trustee: First, the trustee must always take care to be aware of and avoid real or potential conflicts of interest—and the appearance of conflicts of interest—and to disclose any potential conflicts of interest that might have an impact on how he or she makes a decision. Second, the trustee must maintain the strict confidentiality of any and all matters that are confidential.

Conflicts of Interest

The duty of loyalty requires that a trustee be conscious of the potential for a conflict of interest—and to act with candor and care in dealing with such situations. When a conflict of interest—or even a potential conflict of interest—does arise, the trustee must disclose the conflict or potential conflict prior to any discussion of the decision to be made. Preferably, the disclosure should be in writing and given to the secretary of the board. Written disclosure will provide some protection to a trustee who is later challenged on whether the proper disclosure was made.

In addition, any trustee with an actual or potential conflict of interest should abstain from participating in the discussion or vote on the issue in question. If the trustee does not recognize that an agenda item poses a real or potential conflict of interest until the discussion is already under way, he or she should immediately ask for the floor and disclose the newly discovered conflict. In all cases, the trustee should leave the room until the item has been fully discussed and decided. The minutes of the meeting should document that trustee's actions: "Ms. Jones left the room and did not participate in the discussion or vote on the issue because of a conflict of interest."

EXAMPLES

■ Ms. Jones has a brother who would like to be elected to the board of directors of the church daycare program, and he has been working behind the scenes to get his name on the ballot. He has also asked Ms. Jones to help him with her colleague board members. (Appropriate response: Ms. Jones should advise the board that she has a conflict of interest and leave the room and not participate in the discussion or vote regarding her brother. She also should refrain from putting in a plug for her brother with her colleague board members.)

■ Mr. Smith has a financial interest in an insurance brokerage firm that has approached the board about buying its insurance through the firm.

(Appropriate response: Mr. Smith should advise the board that he has a conflict of interest and leave the room and not participate in the discussion or vote regarding the insurance brokerage firm.)

■ Ms. Doe owns five thousand shares of stock in a particular company, and the board is voting on whether to buy a substantial portion of that company's stock with the monies from a new bequest. (Appropriate response: This example does not have a clear-cut answer, but Ms. Doe probably should take the road of caution and advise the board that there is a potential conflict of interest or a perception of conflict of interest. This disclosure alone ordinarily will be sufficient, without the necessity of Ms. Doe leaving the room, because everyone will be on notice that her vote may be affected, even in some small way, by her personal ownership of stock. If Ms. Doe is concerned about whether she can be objective, she should leave the room and not participate in the discussion or vote regarding the purchase of this company's stock. The appropriate response will vary from one situation to another, depending on whether Ms. Doe's ownership of stock in the particular company is sizeable enough to have an impact on her ability to be objective. In some situations the ownership is immaterial, such as in the case of an individual who may own small amounts of stock in many companies through a mutual fund portfolio.)

■ Mr. Lake, who was denied a loan from First Bank two years ago because of some problems in his credit history, has remained angry with the bank for its decision. The church is deciding whether to switch its business from Second Bank to First Bank. (Appropriate response: This example does not have a clear-cut answer and reflects the not-uncommon problem of personal bias that everyone faces from time to time in making decisions. If Mr. Lake is going to stay in the room and participate in the discussion, he probably should advise the board of his personal situation, including the honest disclosure that his feelings about First Bank may or may not be altogether rational and objective.)

Certain types of conflicts of interest cannot be resolved simply by disclosing them and then leaving the room.

EXAMPLES

■ Ms. Invest, a board trustee, is an account manager at the investment firm used by the board to handle its substantial investments. It may be difficult for Ms. Invest to resolve this serious conflict of interest simply by leaving the room for every investment discussion and decision. In all likelihood, she would not be in the room for a significant portion of most meetings. When serious conflicts of interest such as this one exist, Ms. Invest will need to make a choice: either leave the board or divest herself entirely from the outside interest that is causing the conflict.

■ Mr. Estate, a board trustee and commercial real estate broker, is trying to convince the board to sell a prime vacant parcel of land for office condominiums and to allow him to be the broker for the sale. This is a serious conflict of interest for Mr. Estate. He should either resign from the board in order to serve as the broker for this sale or refrain from participating in the entire matter—including both the decision to sell the property and participation as broker in the sale.

Certain types of conflicts of interest cannot be resolved simply by disclosing them and then leaving the room.

The *Discipline* contemplates certain types of conflicts of interest that cannot be resolved by disclosure. For example, ¶¶ 710.6 and 710.7 address and
provide rules for preventing serious conflicts of interest for individuals who
serve on general agencies. These are excellent rules to use for other types of
organizations and boards, even where the *Discipline* is silent.

Courts often deal harshly with those who deal for their own benefit in a
trust situation. Justice Benjamin Cardozo, in the case of Meinhard v. Salmon,
249 N.Y. 458, 464 (1928), made a now-famous and often-quoted statement
concerning the high standards that trustees must uphold:

> Many forms of conduct permissible in a workaday world for those acting at
> arm's length, are forbidden to those bound by fiduciary ties. A trustee is held
> to something stricter than the morals of the market place. Not honesty
> alone, but the punctilio of an honor the most sensitive, is then the standard
> of behavior. As to this there has developed a tradition that is unbending and
> inveterate. Uncompromising rigidity has been the attitude of courts of
> equity when petitioned to undermine the rule of undivided loyalty....

This statement highlights the seriousness with which courts look at
potential breaches of loyalty on the part of trustees. Some people believe that
the courts will not deal as harshly with those who breach this standard in a
religious organization, since the courts in general dislike judicial intrusions
into the affairs of churches.

Beware. The courts in today's world are likely to find self-dealing by
religious leaders to be just as intolerable as any other type of self-dealing,
especially in light of the media attention that has been focused on serious
financial wrongdoing in several religious organizations in recent years.

In summary, a trustee (anyone with a fiduciary responsibility) is strictly
prohibited from making any decision that is—or may have the appearance of
being—in her or his own best interests rather than in the best interests of the
organization or group on whose behalf she or he is making a decision.

Confidentiality

The duty of confidentiality is also an easy one to understand. A trustee
must not disclose information about the organization's activities unless the
information is already known by the public or becomes a matter of public
record. A trustee is not a spokesperson for the board or organization, unless
specifically given that role for a particular purpose.

This duty can be especially important for United Methodists because
of the open/closed meeting rule in ¶ 721 of the *Discipline*. Trustees should
carefully consider whether to call for a closed meeting, pursuant to the
requirements and limitations of ¶ 721, when addressing confidential agenda
items. And, when a meeting is closed pursuant to ¶ 721, it is important to
wait to distribute confidential documents until after the meeting has been
closed, because any document disseminated in an open meeting shall be considered public under this disciplinary requirement.

The *Discipline* also requires that a report on the results of a closed session
is to be made "immediately upon its conclusion or as soon thereafter as is
practicable" (¶ 721, 1996 *Discipline*). It is important that the trustees consider
the nature of such a report prior to reopening the session (for example, who

will make the report, what will be included in the content of the report, and when the report be will made). This type of discussion also will serve as a useful guide for all the trustees on what they should and should not say when asked by friends, colleagues, and others about the action taken. The minutes of the meeting also need to reflect the closed session. (For example, "In accordance with ¶ 721 of the *Discipline,* the [committee/board] by a three-fourths vote of all members present at the meeting voted to close the session, for the purposes of discussing one of the topics provided in ¶ 721. Upon completion of that discussion, the open session was resumed and the [committee/board] announced that…".) No more than the report of the results of the closed session should be reported in the published minutes of the meeting.

Duty of Care

The second primary duty of all trustees is the duty of care. This duty means that a trustee is obligated to act in the best interests of the organization at all times. This obligation is straightforward and easy to understand if the trustee asks him or herself one question before making any decision: *What would be the best decision under the circumstances for this organization at this time and place?* Another way to look at this obligation is for the trustee to ask him or herself: *How would I act if this were my parents' money—or my own assets—at stake in this decision?*

The duty of care has three basic components: First, a trustee must be reasonably informed about an issue before making a decision. Second, a trustee must act as a reasonably prudent person would act under the same or similar circumstances. Third, the trustee must use independent judgment in reaching decisions.

Reasonably Informed

The duty to be reasonably informed means that board members or trustees should not make decisions without adequate information. They should read and understand agenda materials, ask questions, and request more information or time if needed in order to be reasonably informed.

The duty to be informed also means that board members or trustees should be diligent in attending meetings. Board members who do not have time to attend meetings should resign from the board. Also, they should not simply show up and remain silent. Every board member has something to contribute to the group and should make an effort to contribute his or her special gifts. No one person has all of the knowledge or understanding needed to make the wisest decisions for the organization.

The duty to be informed also means that board members should request and receive regular reports on the investment and administration of funds. A board cannot carry out its fiduciary responsibility without timely and accurate information.

Reasonably Prudent

This duty means that a board member should act with such care as a reasonably prudent person would act under similar circumstances in the management of his or her own affairs. This duty also means always acting in good

¶ 721. Closed Session—

In the spirit of openness and accountability, all meetings of councils, boards, agencies, commissions, and committees of the Church, including subunit meetings and teleconferences, shall be open. Portions of a meeting may be closed for consideration of specific subjects if such a closed session is authorized by an affirmative public vote with at least three fourths of the voting members present. The vote shall be taken in public session and recorded in the minutes. Documents distributed in open meetings shall be considered public.

Great restraint should be used in closing meetings; closed sessions should be used as seldom as possible. Subjects that may be considered in closed session are limited to real estate matters; negotiations, when general knowledge could be harmful to the negotiation process; personnel matters; issues related to the accreditation or approval of institutions; discussions relating to litigation or collective bargaining; deployment of security personnel or devices; negotiations involving confidential third-party information; and deliberations of the Judicial Council.

A report on the results of a closed session shall be made immediately upon its conclusion or as soon thereafter as is practicable.

1996 Discipline

Given the facts available at the time of the decision, a board member is required to use his or her best judgment in making a decision.

faith. Good faith means following your conscience. If a board member has information that would be important for other colleagues to know in reaching a decision, he or she should disclose that information. Knowingly remaining silent is not an act of good faith. Given the facts available at the time of the decision, a board member is required to use his or her best judgment in making a decision. Board members are not held responsible for facts they could not have known at the time the decision was made. Decisions made in good faith and with reasonable care should be upheld by a court if challenged in a litigation context.

Board members are not required to make the best decision in all cases. The courts readily acknowledge that trustees are humans who will make mistakes from time to time. Board members are "forgiven" for mistakes as long as they are reasonably informed in making their decisions, act in good faith, participate in the decision-making process, and use independent judgment in reaching their decisions. However, the fact that board members may be "forgiven" for mistakes is not a license to make bad decisions, and it is not an excuse for negligent performance of duties.

Independent Judgment

Board members are not absolved from their fiduciary duty by delegating their responsibility to others. While it is appropriate to rely on the information and expertise of others (such as staff, outside advisors, and others who may have special information or expertise on a particular matter), a board member must reasonably believe that the source of information is reliable and competent and must exercise his or her own independent judgment in evaluating the merits of the information.

For example, a board that is entrusted with a large sum of money may—and in some cases should—engage an investment advisor to assist with investment decisions. However, the board still has the ultimate responsibility for the funds, even if the investment advisor is given broad powers to make investments on behalf of the body. And the board needs to take care that the investment advisor is properly selected and then evaluated on a regular basis (usually annually or biannually). People who are engaged to handle funds should be trustworthy and competent in the areas in which they are being engaged.

In addition, any board member who has any reason to believe that someone in the organization or on the board has committed some financial wrongdoing has a duty to investigate the situation to find out whether there is in fact something inappropriate occurring. A board member who is in this situation should be careful not to slander anyone by accusations of theft or other wrongdoing, but should take steps to find out whether there is any truth to the reasonable suspicion. If a trustee has any questions about how to proceed based on a hunch or suspicion, he or she should confer with legal counsel for assistance.

Likewise, if a board member has reason to believe that funds are being handled sloppily, proper reporting of investments is not being made, or funds are being expended contrary to the organization's (or General Conference's) guidelines, he or she has a duty to inquire why proper actions are not being taken.

Multiple Roles

Many church leaders sit on various boards by virtue of their position as bishop, district superintendent, president of a women's organization, and so forth. These board positions carry the same weight of responsibility as any other board position for which an individual might be elected to serve because of his or her own special interest or expertise.

This means that the board member of a national or global church organization, college, or foundation who is elected because of his or her position owes a fiduciary duty to that organization, as well as to the organization the board member is representing. For example, if the chairperson of the local church finance committee also serves by virtue of his or her position as a member of the board of the community ecumenical food bank, he or she would have a fiduciary responsibility to both the local church and the food bank. An overarching duty is owed to the United Methodist denomination, which rarely, though occasionally, may result in tugs at loyalty. These multiple roles can, quite innocently, create conflicting loyalties, favoritism, opportunities for using one's position on a board to garner support for a favorite personal cause "back home," or benign neglect from having too many board positions. The law does not excuse a person with fiduciary responsibility from his or her duty of loyalty or duty of care. Personal interests, favoritism, dueling loyalties, anger, or neglect have no place when one is serving in a fiduciary role on a board. Judges and juries are not sympathetic to these problems. Individuals who have too many responsibilities or who cannot continue in a way that serves the best interests of the organization should step down rather than continue in a way that breaches the fiduciary duty.

Expenditures and Investments

Those with fiduciary responsibility in the church generally have broad powers and the ultimate legal responsibility, with regard to actions of the organization and expenditures and investment of funds entrusted to them. Because the church is an extended family, and decisions are often made informally and with the same love and care that decisions are made in one's family, it is easy in a church to become so comfortable that the importance of the fiduciary duty is forgotten. At the same time, the sense of family and belonging can make it easy to forget that serving on a board is important "business" and that the decisions being made should be carefully considered as business decisions. In addition, it is important that those with fiduciary responsibility in the church keep in mind the United Methodist Social Principles as they make decisions on behalf of any given church entity. The *Discipline* encourages decisions to be made in support of the goals outlined in those Social Principles (for example, ¶ 2532.5).

With respect to expenditures and investments, it is important to remember that the use of funds may be unrestricted. In other cases, the use of funds may carry certain restrictions, either from the *Discipline,* from organizational rules, from restrictions given by donors, or based on secular law. It is imperative that trustees know and understand the restrictions on the use of funds. Here are some common examples:

■ Paragraph 2542 of the *Discipline* prohibits using proceeds from the sale of a church building for current or budget expenses of a local church.

¶ 2532. Board of Trustees' Powers and Limitations—

5. Subject to the direction of the charge conference as hereinbefore provided, the board of trustees shall receive and administer all bequests made to the local church; shall receive and administer all trusts; and shall invest all trust funds of the local church in conformity with laws of the country, state, or like political unit in which the local church is located....

The board of trustees is encouraged to invest in institutions, companies, corporations, or funds that make a positive contribution toward the realization of the goals outlined in the Social Principles of our Church. The board of trustees is to act as a socially responsible investor and to report annually to the charge conference regarding its carrying out of this responsibility.

1996 Discipline

¶ 2542. Restriction on Proceeds of Mortgage or Sale—

1. No real property on which a church building or parsonage is located shall be mortgaged to provide for the current (or budget) expense of a local church, nor shall the principal proceeds of a sale of any such property be so used. This provision shall apply alike to unincorporated and incorporated local churches.

1996 Discipline

¶ 2503. Trust Clauses in Deeds—

1. Except in conveyances that require that the real property so conveyed shall revert to the grantor if and when its use as a place of divine worship has been terminated, all written instruments of conveyance by which premises are held or hereafter acquired for use as a place of divine worship for members of The United Methodist Church or for other church activities shall contain the following trust clause:

In trust, that said premises shall be used, kept, and maintained as a place of divine worship of the United Methodist ministry and members of The United Methodist Church; subject to the Discipline, *usage, and ministerial appointments of said Church as from time to time authorized and declared by the General Conference and by the annual conference within whose bounds the said premises are situated. This provision is solely for the benefit of the grantee, and the grantor reserves no right or interest in said premises.*

1996 *Discipline*

■ Paragraph 2503 requires that United Methodist property be held in trust for the denomination.

■ Where donors have restricted the use of a fund to a particular purpose—or have stated that only the income may be expended—a board that has agreed to accept the gift is legally bound to administer it according to the donor's restrictions (unless the donor's restrictions are illegal, contrary to public policy, or impossible to carry out). For example, a bequest dedicated to the development of Sunday school curriculum materials for elementary-age children may not be diverted to use for other purposes, such as administrative expenses, college scholarships, or the purchase of a new organ.

Boards should periodically review (on a regular schedule, such as annually or biannually) the administration of donor-restricted funds to ensure that the funds are being handled in accordance with the restrictions. It is the board that ultimately is responsible for the appropriate use of the gifts. Use of funds contrary to a donor's restrictions is a breach of fiduciary duty (except in extraordinary circumstances, such as illegality or impossibility). Boards should assure that restricted and unrestricted funds (including designated funds) are accounted for separately.

Some proposed gifts and bequests are so encumbered with restrictions that administration is extremely costly, difficult, or even impossible. A board has the authority to accept or reject proposed gifts, and rejection should be considered when a board anticipates significant problems in administering a highly restricted gift or bequest.

Breach of Duty

What happens when a trustee breaches his or her fiduciary duty? In a worst-case scenario, when a trustee has knowledge of wrongdoing and fails to act, has a significant conflict of interest and fails to disclose the conflict or recuse (remove) him or herself from participation in a decision, or knows that the board is making a huge mistake and fails to say anything to fellow trustees that would assist them in avoiding the mistake, then the trustee may be exposed to individual, personal liability if there is a lawsuit challenging the board's decision. (For example, if a trustee has knowledge that one of the organization's major investments is about to go sour and fails to disclose that information to the board, costing the organization hundreds of thousands of dollars, then that trustee may be held personally liable for this failure to disclose important information that would have assisted the board in making a proper decision that would have saved the investment dollars.)

Trustees should not spend their time worrying about their potential personal liability exposure, because this type of worrying can interfere with a trustee's ability to do the job with ease and comfort. However, trustees should always be mindful that they have a higher duty of responsibility than the ordinary public and, in essence, are obligated to be good stewards with the church's money. Trustees must always be attentive to the high degree of trust and responsibility they share with their denominational staff in regard to the stewardship of church funds. Their actions affect not only church members but also those who depend upon their organization's charitable services and suffer when those services are diminished. It is your job to set the tone at the top.

Chapter Four

Important Areas of Board Responsibility

Finances, Incorporation, Dealing With Conflict, Insurance

When you walk through fire you shall not be burned, and the flame shall not consume you. (Isaiah 43:2)

And what does the LORD require of you but to do justice, and to love kindness, and to walk humbly with your God? (Micah 6:8)

Financial Responsibilities

Many people who serve on the boards of church organizations are not financial experts. This may be their first experience with reviewing statements of financial position (balance sheets), making cash-flow projections, setting adequate reserves, or monitoring cash flow and budgets. Not everyone on a board needs to be a financial expert. Each person brings unique gifts to the board table. Each board member must ensure, however, that the board as a whole is adequately managing and protecting the organization's finances and that good stewardship is exercised in the use of funds. Increasingly, donors are asking questions of stewardship, questions of balance between administrative and program costs. Donors want more and more information and have come to expect a high level of accountability. A great example of how large charitable organizations are responding to these donor expectations is the Web site (http://www.guidestar.org) developed by Philanthropic Research, Inc. of Williamsburg, Virginia, where the annual 990 tax returns of charities are being published.

While most religious organizations are not obligated to file Form 990, donors are nonetheless looking for this same type of accountability and good stewardship. In fact, the case could be made that self-examination by the boards of religious organizations is even more important, since there is no required accountability to the IRS or other regulatory body.

How can you, as a board member, assure yourself that your organization is accountable to its donors and is exercising good stewardship in the use of funds? Here are several musts:

1. Financial information for review and approval by the board should be received well in advance of a board meeting.
   a. Annual audits and management letters should be thoroughly reviewed, and an action plan to remedy any deficiencies adopted by the board.
   b. Annual budgets should reflect a balance of administrative and program expenses and a planned use of current income and reserves.

c. Quadrennial budgets should reflect this same balance, as well as a long-range plan for the board's objectives.

Questions in the area of financial information should include, but not be limited to, the following:

✓ Is cash projected to be adequate?

✓ Are cash-flow projections realistic, reasonable, and objective?

✓ Are reserves adequate?

✓ Where are the investment policies, and is the organization following them?

✓ Where are expenses increasing and why?

✓ How is the budget monitored?

✓ Is income increasing or decreasing? If it is decreasing, what is the board doing about it?

✓ Are expenses under control?

✓ What is the ratio of administrative versus program expenses?

✓ What internal controls are in place to protect expenditures and ensure their propriety?

✓ Are adequate checks and balances in place to prevent errors, fraud, and abuse?

✓ Are the board, management, and auditors alert to the possibility of fraud?

✓ Is the financial staff providing accurate and timely financial statements that help to provide a clear understanding of the financial state of the organization?

✓ Is the bank providing satisfactory services at a reasonable cost?

✓ Has the board made a risk analysis to assure that the risk of loss of money and assets are minimized?

2. All board members should be familiar with board-adopted financial policies and procedures. Questions in the area of financial policies should include, but not be limited to, the following:

✓ Is the reserves policy current and appropriate?

✓ What are the investment policies, and is the organization following them?

✓ Who monitors the financial policies?

✓ How often are financial policies reviewed?

✓ In areas where the *Discipline* or GCFA provide basic standards, are board policies and practices consistent with those standards?

3. Questions in the area of financial staffing should include, but not be limited to, the following:

✓ Do we have adequately trained staff in both professional skills and church financial culture?

✓ Does the staff demonstrate credibility?

✓ Is there adequate separation of financial responsibility?

✓ Is the staff able to provide the board with reasonable answers to questions and data to back up those answers?

4. Matters of financial impropriety should be disclosed to the full board with an outline of how policies and procedures will be changed to prevent or reduce the potential of a reoccurrence.

Board members may always ask for help. Asking good questions is a crucial board role.

It is important to note that boards should not micromanage the day-to-day operations of the organization. Micromanaging is inefficient, hurts staff morale, and leads to an ineffective organization. Micromanaging staff can also lead to legal problems when a board gets involved in personnel matters beyond the CEO/board relationship. For example, the board should not direct the CEO (also known in many United Methodist organizations as the general secretary or executive director) to terminate a particular staff person who, at the moment, is unpopular with the board. In a staff downsizing, the board should set downsizing policies and approve a downsizing plan but should not direct the CEO to save "favorite" staff persons and terminate others. The board also should not conduct the annual performance evaluations for any staff except those who report directly to the board.

A balance exists between an overly passive, uninvolved, uninformed board and one that micromanages. An appropriately active board sets policy, asks sufficient questions to determine whether existing policies are being met and whether new policies are needed, obtains the information it needs in response to questions, evaluates the organization's performance, ensures that the organization's assets are adequately protected, and understands and appreciates the day-to-day operational role of staff.

EXAMPLE

The example regarding the Santa Clara United Way (page 11) illustrates the importance of asking questions about the organization's finances. In that instance, an organization with ample reserves and a clean budget had in five years used up its reserves and was operating in a serious deficit. It was then unable to meet its funding commitments to charities that depended on its funding for their own survival. Had the board asked the above questions and engaged in an ongoing evaluation of its governance (see Chapter One), it probably would not have spiraled downward in this manner.

What About Incorporating?

Volunteer leaders and staff of church organizations and congregations frequently ask if incorporation of the organization is a good idea and, if so, how it can be accomplished. As a general statement and where local laws permit, incorporation can be advantageous, both to protect individual trustees/directors from personal liability for the acts or omissions of the organization and to provide an entity with continuous existence for purposes of ownership of real property.

Because incorporation is controlled by state statutes, church organizations considering incorporating should consult local legal counsel, in order to properly set up and structure the corporate entity, in compliance with the *Discipline* and in compliance with state law requirements. Many states have a not-for-profit incorporation statute, which simplifies the process of incorporation and traditional requirements for the filing of annual reports. In general, fees are also lower when not-for-profit incorporation statutes are used.

An appropriately active board sets policy, asks sufficient questions to determine whether existing policies are being met and whether new policies are needed, obtains the information it needs in response to questions, evaluates the organization's performance, ensures that the organization's assets are adequately protected, and understands and appreciates the day-to-day operational role of staff.

In some states, the individual board members can be sued for the liabilities of the organization if the organization is not incorporated.

For example, the General Council on Finance and Administration (GCFA) of The United Methodist Church is incorporated under the Illinois law. Each year, GCFA files an annual report with the Illinois secretary of state, listing the directors and officers and corporate purpose, as well as the agent for service of any legal papers upon the corporation. Annual filing fees are nominal, increasing slightly when changes in address or agent are included.

One of the primary advantages of incorporating is in limiting liability for acts of the corporation to the assets of the corporation. In general, the personal finances of individual corporate directors are not in jeopardy due to litigation against the organization unless the directors have defrauded the church by embezzlement, self-dealing, and so forth. In some states, the individual board members can be sued for the liabilities of the organization if the organization is not incorporated. Even in states where an unincorporated organization can be sued—which lowers the risk that the individual board members will be sued—plaintiffs' attorneys, in general, feel more comfortable that they have correctly identified and named the organization if it is incorporated and the name can be checked with the state. If they cannot readily identify and name the unincorporated organization—or are concerned about the viability of a lawsuit against an unincorporated organization—they are likely, as a precaution, to name the individual board members as defendants. This type of overzealous lawyering can be avoided in most cases when the organization is incorporated and thus readily identifiable through the state authorities as a viable organization.

The other main advantage of incorporation is establishment of a permanent continuing entity to hold title to church property.

The primary disadvantage of incorporation is the modest administrative hassle: complying with the state's not-for-profit corporation laws and complying with the state law requirements of the necessary paperwork for incorporation, filing fees, annual reports.

Each church organization needs to make the decision, in consultation with legal counsel, to incorporate (or not) based on its own unique needs and circumstances. GCFA's legal department (847-869-3345, ext. 6701) has sample United Methodist local church bylaws and articles of incorporation, together with charge conference resolutions, for the local church that is considering incorporation. In addition, United Methodist church organizations considering incorporation should carefully review ¶¶ 2503, 2506, 2529, 2538, and 2539 of the *Discipline*. It is strongly recommended that the bylaws of the organization state: "This organization is required to comply with *The Book of Discipline of The United Methodist Church—1996*, which is incorporated herein by reference."

Dealing With Conflict

Conflict is a part of the life of every religious organization. All of us have our own examples: the controversy over the new pipe organ, choir robes, or hymnals; the disappointed donor who feels that his or her large donation isn't being used for its intended purposes; the board member who voted no on an important decision and then in frustration told a large group of members why the decision was "wrong"; the disappointment and fears of the members of the church who don't want a rock band playing praise songs in the sanctuary of the church; the staff member whose ideas have been rejected by the board; the angry letters to the pastor about the change in the order of worship or design of the new sign in front of the church property.

If conflict is handled poorly, it can be destructive. If it is handled constructively, religious institutions can be transformed in positive ways.

In general terms, there are three basic ways individuals deal with conflict: fight (battle), flight (avoid), or engage (address openly and collaboratively). We all probably would like to say that we engage conflict openly and collaboratively. More often, however, we have been taught from a young age to battle or avoid conflict. Most people, being completely honest, would have to admit that they would prefer to avoid conflict at all costs. Our attitude toward conflict is important, and it is worth spending time as a board thinking about and engaging in discussion about our individual and collective attitude toward conflict and our typical actions when dealing with conflict.

The Latin root of the English word *conflict* is *confligere*, which means "to strike together." How different this is from the Chinese symbol of conflict, which is a combination of two terms: *danger* and *opportunity*. In reality, conflict is not so much a collision as a challenge. This is indeed the biblical view of conflict, with the Bible being a long story of conflicts that are transformative for those involved.

Conflict is not only a natural part of life, but also can be helpful—if not required—for growth and change. Individuals usually need conflict, as do organizations, for new life. Remember the cross, which is at the center of Christian faith: conflict, estrangement, death and yet forgiveness, grace, reconciliation and new life.

Pastors often say that one basic aspect of their seminary training that was missing was how to deal with conflict. Directors of church organizations can say the same thing. It is easy to give and receive awards, attend banquets, and congratulate staff on their fine work. It is much more difficult—and yet more common—for a board to be facing a thorny issue that includes a conflict or a potential conflict.

Boards should be trained and retrained on handling conflicts in peaceful and collaborative ways that create growth, change, and transformation rather than resentment and destruction. Training opportunities abound and should be explored. Some are focused on church organizations; others are based on business models. The basic teachings are the same, whether based on a biblical or business model. Boards should practice their learnings and serve as a role model for everyone else in the organization on how conflict can be engaged openly and collaboratively for the health and vitality of the organization.

This handbook would be much simpler and shorter if the church and all its people knew how to handle conflict in a positive way and how to establish processes for decision-making that those involved feel are fair. Most conflicts consist of three basic elements: two or more people, a problem, and the process by which decisions are made. These three basic elements should be familiar to all boards because every decision made by a board has the potential for conflict or already involves conflict in some way.

Remember the cross, which is at the center of Christian faith: conflict, estrangement, death and yet forgiveness, grace, reconciliation and new life.

Insurance

Boards are responsible for adequately insuring the organization against those risks of financial loss that could impair the organization's ability to carry out its mission. Insurance is readily available to cover most of those risks, and the cost is manageable because it can be budgeted. What is really expensive and unmanageable is a loss that was either uninsured or underinsured by a wide margin.

Property insurance should be on a "blanket basis" per location, and on an "all risk" replacement cost form. Buy insurance to full replacement cost value. Learn what your property is currently worth. You will be glad you did if a natural disaster occurs.

The risk of litigation in general is on the rise, and church board members are foolishly blind if they think church organizations are immune to litigation. Lawsuits against church organizations are filed by loyal church members, disgruntled members, injured or disappointed guests, and others.

EXAMPLES

- A member or guest who falls down stairs that are in disrepair may sue the church organization, claiming that the church negligently failed to maintain the stairs.

- A youth rafting trip results in a serious injury to a youth who falls out of the raft (could also be a ski outing, canoe trip, lock-in). The youth's family sues the church and the rafting company for negligence, claiming that there was inadequate supervision of the youth on the trip, negligent selection of the rafting company, and negligent hosting of the trip by the rafting company.

- A member is burned by an open-pit fire while participating in group games at the annual church pig roast. The member sues the church for negligence, claiming that the church should have organized the group games in a location away from the fire and should have put barricades around the fire.

- A guest trips on an uneven sidewalk in front of the church. The guest sues the city and the church, claiming that the sidewalk was negligently installed and maintained and that the church lighting created shadows on the sidewalk, making it impossible to see that it was uneven.

- The city is working on the sewers in front of the church and a passerby is injured on pipes. The passerby sues the city, the construction company, and the church, claiming that the church should have erected warning signs on its premises to inform passersby that sewer work was being done on the property.

- A neighborhood child is injured on the church's twenty-year-old playground equipment, which is mounted on a concrete pad. The child's family sues the church for negligence, on the basis that the playground equipment does not meet the current standard of care for playground equipment.

- A well-meaning member of the church council tells a close friend in confidence that the choir director is an emotionally unstable alcoholic who cannot hold a job. The friend repeats to two other close friends the rumor, which is not true. The choir director sues the well-meaning member of the church council, the pastor, and the church for defamation.

- While voluntarily washing windows at the annual church cleanup day, a member falls from a ladder and is seriously injured. The member sues the church, claiming that the ladder was unsafe and that the church should have required a spotter to hold the ladder and prevent it from tipping over.
- The pastor asks a retired member of the church to help with some maintenance and repairs. The member is electrocuted while rewiring the electrical system in the fellowship hall. The member's spouse files a wrongful death lawsuit against the church, claiming that the church was negligent because it should have hired professional electricians instead of asking and allowing volunteers to do work for which they were not professionally qualified.

(Note: These examples are fictitious and are provided for illustrative purposes only. They are not intended to create or suggest a standard of care or to suggest that anyone file a lawsuit against a church organization for these or other problems.)

In recent years, litigation against the directors of some nonprofit organizations has increased. The significance of this risk varies greatly, depending on the size of the organization, who it serves, and what it is responsible for managing. A board member's potential liability in litigation does not arise every time the organization itself may be liable; it arises out of the director's fiduciary duty to the organization (or to a specific party).

EXAMPLES
- A church organization in distress that uses staff pension funds to cover general operating expenses is at great risk of litigation by staff pensioners, against the organization and its board members.
- A staff person alleges sexual harassment by a board member, and the board directs the chief executive officer to terminate the staff person for bringing the complaint.

The board should seek the expertise of an insurance agent or broker who is knowledgeable about the insurance needs of nonprofit organizations in general, and churches in particular. There are many options to consider in the type and amount of coverage. The GCFA United Methodist Insurance Program can provide this kind of assistance.

The board of trustees at the local church is required by the *Discipline* (¶ 2532.2) to conduct an annual review of the adequacy of personnel insurance and of the property, liability, and crime insurance coverage on church-owned property, buildings, and equipment. All church organizations should conduct such an annual review, in consultation with their insurance agents or brokers.

The types of coverage that should be considered in the annual evaluation by all church organizations include:
- property insurance that includes boiler and machinery breakdown coverage
- any special coverage needed for antiques, stained glass, art, special objects, papers and records
- general liability (including sexual misconduct claims)
- auto insurance for hired and non-owned vehicles
- fidelity bond coverage for people who handle money (see, for example, ¶¶ 262.4b, 615.1, 809, 1508.9b, 1626, and 2511 in the *Discipline*)

¶ 2532. Board of Trustees' Powers and Limitations—

2. The board of trustees shall review annually the adequacy of the property, liability, and crime insurance coverage on church-owned property, buildings, and equipment. The board of trustees shall also review annually the adequacy of personnel insurance. The purpose of these reviews is to ensure that the church, its properties, and its personnel are properly protected against risks. The board shall include in its report to the charge conference (¶ 2549.7) the results of its review and any recommendations it deems necessary.

1996 *Discipline*

For more information about the United Methodist Insurance Program, contact the insurance staff of the General Council on Finance and Administration (GCFA) at 847-869-3345, ext. 6748.

- money and securities insurance
- directors and officers liability insurance (D&O) that covers not only the organization but also employees and volunteers
- employment practices liability coverage (even if the pastor is the only paid employee)
- liability coverage for trips and tours inside and outside of the United States
- pastoral counseling liability insurance

It is important that the board discuss all aspects of the organization's activities with the insurance agent or broker, to ensure there is the optimum amount of coverage for all activities of the church (preschool, annual youth mission trip, homeless shelter, foundation, vacation Bible school, a camp, nursing home, parent's day-out program, counseling service, rental of premises, third-party use of premises, annual festival, rafting trips, bazaars, and so forth). Make sure the liability policies include as insureds both the paid staff and the volunteers.

In summary, insurance companies do not like surprises. They need to know what risks they are insuring against, and boards need to know what risks they are protecting with their insurance premiums.

The General Council on Finance and Administration is prepared to discuss The United Methodist Insurance Program and the insurance needs of your organization. For more information, contact GCFA's insurance staff (847-869-3345, ext. 6748).

Chapter Five

Litigation Do's and Don'ts

If another member of the church sins against you, go and point out the fault when the two of you are alone. If the member listens to you, you have regained that one. But if you are not listened to, take one or two others along with you, so that every word may be confirmed by the evidence of two or three witnesses. If the member refuses to listen to them, tell it to the church; and if the offender refuses to listen even to the church, let such a one be to you as a Gentile and a tax collector. (Matthew 18:15-17)

A lawsuit has been filed against your church and you naturally panic. It is frightening and intimidating to be sued. It can happen to you at any time and for any or no reason. These practical tips are designed to help local churches handle lawsuits with the savvy of an expert. Take a deep breath, stay calm, and read on.

When the Papers Arrive

✓ Do not sign anything other than a simple messenger's receipt that acknowledges your receipt of court papers.

✓ Keep the envelope or wrappers in which the papers arrived.

✓ Make a written notation of the date and time the documents were received and the method by which they were received (hand delivery by a court official, mail, other). Be specific.

✓ Call your attorney immediately for instructions. (If you don't have an attorney, call an attorney who is a member of your congregation for assistance on what to do next. Your insurance broker or agent also can be helpful.)

✓ Call your insurance broker or agent immediately, and forward a copy of the papers to him or her with a dated cover letter. (Save a copy of the cover letter.) Inquire whether this is the type of lawsuit that will be covered by your liability insurance. If it is, find out when and how an attorney will be retained to represent you. If it is unlikely that there will be insurance coverage, then it becomes even more important to seek competent legal counsel immediately. It is advisable to consult with legal counsel even if your insurance company provides one, particularly if the claims seek to recover an amount in excess of your policy limits or if your insurance carrier issues a "reservation of rights" letter.

✓ Determine whether your church has a policy already in place for what to do when a lawsuit is filed. If it does, make sure you follow the requirements outlined in such a policy.

✓ Deliver a copy of the papers to other leaders in your congregation or organization, as appropriate (for example, the chairperson of the staff/pastor parish relations committee, the treasurer, the chairperson of the church council, and so forth).

✓ Inform the district superintendent or bishop, as appropriate.

✓ Inform your annual conference chancellor, as appropriate.

✓ If the complaint names The United Methodist Church, a bishop, the Council of Bishops, the General Conference, or any general agency as a defendant, immediately contact GCFA's legal department (847-869-3345, ext. 6701). The United Methodist Church is the name of the denomination, but it is not a jural entity capable of being sued.

The Next Step

✓ Sit down immediately with your attorney and a small group of leaders to discuss key strategy issues. (The group will vary depending on the nature of the lawsuit. It might include people such as the chairperson of the church council, the pastor, the district superintendent, the lay leader, and the person who knows the most about the particular situation.)

✓ Prepare for possible media interest. (Read *Not If, But When! A Crisis Manual,* which is listed on page 43 in this book.)

✓ Decide who is going to be the "up-front" person on the lawsuit to handle inquiries, assist counsel, follow what's happening, and so forth. This person should be someone who has excellent follow-through skills, knows how to keep information in strict confidence, and consistently uses good judgment about delicate matters. Ensure that this person gets the training he or she needs regarding what is appropriate to say, when, and to whom. (Consult your attorney for advice on this.)

✓ Consider whether this is a case that can be mediated. Is Christian reconciliation possible?

✓ Ensure that a good file of all documents is maintained, and decide who is going to maintain and be responsible for that file. To assure that the attorney-client and other privileges are protected and that documents are not inadvertently misplaced, limit access to the file after consultation with your attorney.

✓ Decide whether the local church congregation (or other church organization) needs to be informed of the lawsuit, as applicable, and how much they should be told. (Again, be careful; seek legal advice. It is important to be open with the local congregation, if it is possible to do so without increasing the church's potential liability exposure.)

✓ Decide whether any local church pastoral care will be needed, and develop a plan to address those needs.

✓ Decide whether pastoral care will be important for anyone else, including yourself.

✓ If the lawsuit is based on some type of clergy misconduct, determine whether there has been an internal disciplinary action filed and, if so, what its status is. If not, decide whether it would be appropriate to pursue such an action at this time. (Again, be careful; seek legal advice.)

✓ Make sure an attorney is hired immediately to file the appropriate response to the lawsuit. If your insurance agent/broker is not able to give you the name, address, and phone number of the attorney assigned to the case within several days of your receipt of the papers, you will need to have your own attorney obtain an extension of time for the filing of appropriate papers. Important, short deadlines exist for the filing of responses in lawsuits, and filing the wrong response can result in significant legal problems down the line. It is crucial that an attorney be on the alert immediately to protect your interests.

✓ Do not talk with anyone about the lawsuit, except your attorney and the small group of leaders who will work together to develop a strategy for what to do next.

✓ Do not call the plaintiff, his or her attorney, or anyone else who might be on the other side in this matter.

✓ Do not—at any time or for any reason—call, write, or visit with the judge.

✓ Ask your attorney before you act.

✓ Remind yourself, your attorney, and others that this is a church and that a church is different from other parties in a civil lawsuit. It is important for the church to act as a church at all times.

When You Meet With Your Attorney

✓ Be completely open, truthful, and forthright. Your attorney cannot help you if you hide information. Do not try to decide what information is important or unimportant; let your attorney be the judge of that. Tell everything you know.

✓ Bring a copy of all documents, writings, and things that may have anything to do with the lawsuit. Keep the originals in a safe place.

✓ Talk with your attorney about your insurance coverage.

✓ Remind your attorney that she or he represents you, not your insurance carrier.

✓ Listen to your attorney and follow his or her advice. If you disagree with something your attorney says, tell him or her that you disagree and then iron out the issue right then and there.

✓ Educate your attorney about the United Methodist denomination. Make sure that he or she understands the importance of the structure of The United Methodist Church. Tell your attorney that there are lawyers at GCFA who may have legal research, briefs, and other helpful materials that would be of assistance in the case.

✓ If you receive a "reservation of rights" letter or a "denial of coverage" letter from your insurance carrier, you should obtain an opinion from your annual conference chancellor or a special insurance coverage attorney about whether there are steps you should take to protect your legal rights under the insurance policy (or policies). Letters of this type are sent directly from the insurance carrier and should be discussed promptly with your selected legal counsel and not with the one provided by the insurance carrier.

As the Case Progresses

✓ Review and follow the advice in the previous sections.

✓ Call your attorney immediately if you receive any additional official papers related to the lawsuit.

✓ Make sure your "up-front" person is continually updated about the status of the case and has access to independent legal counsel (such as the conference chancellor) to help answer questions about legal strategies and maneuverings and to address concerns regarding insurance coverage or actions being taken in the lawsuit by your attorney or others.

✓ Try to be patient. The court system is sometimes slow and cumbersome, and it may seem as if it is taking forever for your case to get anywhere. This, too, shall pass.

Chapter Six

Taxation

"Teacher, we know that you teach the truth about what God wants people to do. And you treat everyone with the same respect, no matter who they are. Tell us, should we pay taxes to the Emperor or not?" Jesus knew that they were trying to trick him. So he told them, "Show me a coin." Then he asked, "Whose picture and name are on it?" "The Emperor's," they answered. Then he told them, "Give the Emperor what belongs to him and give God what belongs to God." (Luke 20:21-25, CEV)

Board members should have a basic understanding of the tax status of the organization they serve and the basic do's and don'ts regarding the application of the tax laws to the organization. This section will outline the primary federal income tax issues that apply to church organizations.

Exemption

Most United Methodist church organizations qualify for tax-exempt status under Section 501(c)(3) of the Internal Revenue Code. In order to qualify for exemption as a 501(c)(3) organization, the organization must be organized and operated exclusively for charitable, religious, educational, literary, or scientific purposes. See IRS Publication 557 ("Tax-Exempt Status for Your Organization"), which is on the IRS Web site (http://www. irs.gov).

The General Council on Finance and Administration of The United Methodist Church (GCFA) maintains a group 501(c)(3) tax exemption for all local United Methodist churches, annual conferences, and general agencies. Many other United Methodist church organizations qualify for participation in the Group Ruling that GCFA maintains. (Examples include annual conference foundations, local church preschools, and the like.) For more information about the Group Ruling and who may benefit from it, contact GCFA's legal department (847-869-3345, ext. 6701) or visit GCFA's Web site (http://www.gcfa.org).

The two primary advantages of tax exemption for church organizations are that the church organization is exempt from most federal income taxes, and donations are tax-deductible.

In order to operate as tax-exempt, church organizations must comply with certain basic rules:

- The organization must be organized and operated exclusively for tax-exempt purposes.
- It must not carry on substantial activities to influence legislation.
- It must never participate in any political campaign. (A detailed memo explaining this rule is available from GCFA's legal department at 847-869-3345, ext. 6701. Or visit GCFA's Web site at http://www.gcfa.org.)
- The organization's activities must not be for the benefit of any private or personal interests of any individual (called "private inurement").

While most of the income of church organizations is exempt from federal taxation, the Internal Revenue Code imposes a tax on income that is "unrelated" to the organization's exempt purpose. This tax is known as the Unrelated Business Income Tax (UBIT). IRS Publication 598 ("Tax on Unrelated Business Income of Exempt Organizations"), which is available on the IRS Web site (http://www.irs.gov), gives more detailed information on this tax.

The Internal Revenue Code defines unrelated business income as income derived from an activity that is "regularly carried on" and that is "not substantially related" to the organization's exempt purpose. For example, a church that sells candy twice a year to raise funds for a youth mission trip probably is not engaged in an activity that is regularly carried on. If a church opens a candy store that is in competition with the local candy franchise operation, the church is engaged in an activity that is regularly carried on. Whether the candy store operation is unrelated to the church's mission and ministry and thus generating unrelated business income (that would be subject to UBIT) is a more-complex question. The point of this example is to highlight the need for board members to recognize the potential UBIT issues with any new revenue-generating activities that are regularly carried on, and to seek competent advice from a nonprofit tax advisor on the potential tax implications of these activities.

In general, the Internal Revenue Code excludes certain otherwise unrelated income from UBIT:

- dividends, interest, payments with respect to securities, loans, and annuities
- royalties
- most rents from real property (unless the property is debt-financed, in which case a whole new set of rules apply)
- gain from the sale of capital assets
- certain research income

Again, a church organization contemplating new sources of revenue should seek competent advice from a nonprofit tax advisor. With good tax advice and structuring, it may be possible to minimize the risk of revenue being classified as unrelated.

Church organizations with substantial revenue from activities that might be unrelated should consider establishing a for-profit subsidiary corporation for the activity. An exempt organization can risk its exempt status if its unrelated business generates substantial income, making the church organization appear to be more of a for-profit business than a charitable organization. Again, careful tax planning and advice is essential.

Charitable Contributions

The Revenue Reconciliation Act of 1993 includes significant new changes regarding the reporting requirements for charities to taxpayers and taxpayers to the IRS on certain charitable contributions and gifts. For the typical Sunday morning contribution of cash or check of less than $250, there are no reporting changes or substantiation changes for the taxpayer. The canceled check or receipt from the donee church showing the church name and the amount and dates of the contribution are still sufficient for this type of contribution. However, if there are individual cash or check contributions of $250 or more, or if non-cash property worth $250 or more is donated, there are substantial requirements. In addition, there are quid pro quo rules that apply to contributions of $75 or more that are part contribution and part payment for goods or services in exchange for the contribution (for example, a purchase of a $100 ticket to a fundraising event such as a dinner/dance).

For more information about charitable deductions, see IRS Publication 526 ("Charitable Contributions"), which is available at the IRS Web site (http://www.irs.gov).

Substantiation Rules

Starting in 1994, donors who make a contribution of $250 or more must have "contemporaneous written acknowledgment from the donee organization" (IRS Publication 526). A canceled check will no longer be sufficient to substantiate a contribution of this size. A written document from the church (including the church's name or on church letterhead) should be provided to meet the new requirements. This document must be in the donor's hands prior to the date on which the donor's tax return is filed or prior to the due date for filing, whichever is earlier. This document must include:

- the name of the donor
- a list including each individual contribution of $250 or more (Churches are not required to aggregate smaller contributions that add up to $250 or more in order to trigger these new requirements.)
- a statement that no goods or services were provided to the donor in exchange for the contribution. GCFA would suggest that all church statements reflecting money contributions, such as quarterly giving reports, state the following:
  Pursuant to Internal Revenue Code requirements for substantiation of charitable contributions, (*Church's Name*) United Methodist Church provided no goods or services in return for these contributions. (*You may wish to add:* except intangible religious benefits.)

  a very good idea!
- a description of any non-cash property contributed

Some volunteers, committee members, and directors of church organizations may incur out-of-pocket expenditures in those activities that may qualify for charitable deductions if all substantiation acknowledgment requirements are met. (For example, volunteers who travel to do a work project who bring their own supplies may qualify for a charitable deduction contribution for their travel and other actual expenses.) The IRS unofficially has indicated in pending guidelines that the volunteer may satisfy the substantiation requirement if

- adequate records of expenditures are kept;
- the church organization furnishes a written acknowledgment that services were performed that required the expense (such as travel away from home);
- the written acknowledgment states that no goods or services were provided to the volunteer (or a good-faith estimate of the value of such services).

Quid Pro Quo Rules

Starting in 1994, where goods or services—other than "intangible religious benefits," such as prayers—are provided in return for contributions exceeding $75, the law requires donors to be provided a written statement "in connection with the solicitation or receipt of the contribution" (IRS Publication 526). GCFA suggests that the church's written acknowledgment of such gifts include the following statement:

> In accordance with Internal Revenue Code requirements, we are required to inform you that the amount of your contributions that is tax-deductible is limited to the amount of the contribution you made less the value of any goods or services we provided in return. The law requires us to furnish you this statement and a good-faith estimate of the value of goods and services provided to you in connection with this gift. The value of the goods or services provided to you is (include amount).

The only exceptions are where the goods are token gift items (such as pens, pencils, and so forth) bearing the church name and valued at $6.20 or less, or where the value of the goods or services is less than the lesser of $62 or 2% of the amount of the contribution.

Form 990 Tax Returns

The general rule is that organizations exempt from taxation under Section 501(a) of the Internal Revenue Code, including Section 501(c)(3) organizations, are required to file annual information returns on Form 990. This form can be downloaded from the IRS Web site (http://www. irs.gov).

The IRS uses the following list of organizational characteristics to determine whether an organization is a church:

- a distinct legal existence
- a recognized creed and form of worship
- a definite and distinct ecclesiastical government
- a formal code of doctrine and discipline
- a distinct religious history
- a membership not associated with any other church or denomination
- an organization of ordained ministers
- ordained ministers selected after completing prescribed courses of study
- a literature of its own
- established places of worship
- regular congregations
- regular religious services
- Sunday schools for religious instruction of the young
- schools for the preparation of its ministers

Contact GCFA's legal department (847-869-3345, ext. 6701) for information regarding the requirements for 990 forms.

New Disclosure Rules

The IRS recently issued new regulations that require local churches and church organizations to make available for public inspection certain records related to their IRS tax exemption. The regulations relate to Section 6104(d) of the Internal Revenue Code and are printed in the Federal

Register (Volume 64; April 9, 1999; pages 17279–91. Effective date: June 8, 1999). The regulations can be found on the Federal Register Web site (http://www.nara.gov/fedreg).

Most United Methodist churches and church organizations are or have elected to be covered by the group tax exemption that is maintained by the General Council on Finance and Administration (GCFA) for the entire denomination. GCFA is the holder of the Group Ruling for the United Methodist denomination. The United Methodist Church is not a jural or legal entity.

All churches and church organizations that are tax-exempt, regardless of whether the tax exemption is through the Group Ruling or a separate tax exemption, must comply with these new regulations. And there are significant monetary penalties for failure to comply.

The regulations require a tax-exempt organization to make its application for exemption available for public inspection without charge at its principal office and at certain regional or district offices. Compliance with these regulations can be accomplished fairly easily. If a United Methodist organization that is covered by the Group Ruling exemption receives a request for disclosure, that organization can promptly contact GCFA's legal department (847-869-3345, ext. 6701), which will provide the proper material.

Since GCFA has been issued and maintains the Group Ruling for the denomination, GCFA is in the best position to provide the information you will need. You should provide the following information when requesting information:

- the original request by GCFA for Group Ruling exemption for the United Methodist denomination
- the IRS's response granting a Group Ruling status
- information specifically naming the organization

For further information or assistance regarding the Group Ruling, contact GCFA's legal department (847-869-3345, ext. 6701).

EXAMPLE

If the ABC Church Organization received a request under this disclosure regulation, ABC should immediately call GCFA's legal department. (The regulations allow a reasonable time—normally two weeks—to respond.) GCFA would then forward to ABC a copy of the original request for a Group Ruling exemption; the October 16, 1974, IRS response; and the page from *General Minutes of the Annual Conferences of The United Methodist Church* on which the ABC Church Organization is listed. Depending on the nature of the request, ABC would then either allow inspection of this material by the individual making the request at the church organization's office or would mail a copy to that individual.

Conclusion

In general, church organizations obtain most of their funds from the generous stewardship of donors. Board members and trustees have a moral and legal duty to protect those funds with the highest degree of skill, competency, and integrity. This means that board members must be knowledgeable about the organization, active in the decision-making process, and loyal to the organization. In short, board members must always act in the best interests of the organization. The actions—and inactions—of the board set the tone at the top for how all others in the organization can and will behave. Trust is at the core. If members lose their trust in the organization's integrity, they will no longer give of their funds, their time, or their spirits; and the overall mission of the church will have failed.

Additional Sources for More Help

Financial Responsibilities of the Nonprofit Board, by Andrew S. Lang (Washington, DC: National Center for Nonprofit Boards, 1998). Internet: http://www.ncnb.org. Phone: 800-883-6262.

Getting to Yes: Negotiating Agreement Without Giving In (Second Edition), by Roger Fisher and William Ury and edited by Bruce Patton (New York: Penguin Books, 1991). Available from most bookstores.

Guidebook for Directors of Nonprofit Corporations, edited by George W. Overton (Chicago: American Bar Association, Section of Business Law, 1993). Internet: http://www.abanet.org. Phone: 800-285-2221.

Healthy Nonprofits: Conserving Scarce Resources Through Effective Internal Controls (Washington, DC: Nonprofit Risk Management Center, 1996). Phone: 202-785-3891.

Internal Control/Internal Audit for the Agencies of The United Methodist Church (Nashville: General Council on Finance and Administration of The United Methodist Church, 1999). Phone: 615-329-3393, ext. 12.

Local Church Audit Guide, by Sandra Kelley Lackore (Nashville: General Council on Finance and Administration of The United Methodist Church, revised October 1998). Internet: http://www.gcfa.org. Phone: 615-329-3393, ext. 12.

1997–2000 Legal Manual (Evanston, IL: General Council on Finance and Administration of The United Methodist Church, 1996). Send a check for $10 to GCFA Legal Department, 1200 Davis Street, Evanston, IL 60201.

Not If, But When! A Crisis Manual (Second Edition), by Floyd A. Craig, under the direction of Alan Griggs (Nashville: United Methodist Communications, 1999). Phone: 800-476-7766.

Ten Basic Responsibilities of Nonprofit Boards, by Richard T. Ingram (Washington, DC: National Center for Nonprofit Boards, revised 1996). Internet: http://www.ncnb.org. Phone: 800-883-6262.

The Promise of Mediation: Responding to Conflict Through Empowerment and Recognition (The Jossey-Bass Conflict Resolution Series), by Robert A. Baruch Bush and Joseph P. Folger (San Francisco: Jossey-Bass Publisher, 1994). Available from most bookstores.

2000 Church & Clergy Tax Guide, by Richard R. Hammar, J.D., LL.M., CPA (Matthews, NC: Christian Ministry Resources, 1999). Internet: http://www.iclonline.com. Phone: 800-222-1840.

Glossary of Terms

Articles of Incorporation

The basic written instrument that is filed with the appropriate governmental body (commonly the secretary of state at the state government level) establishing the incorporation of an organization. The contents of this document are usually prescribed by state law and typically include such things as the name of the organization, its purpose and power, its period of existence, and any conditions on its operation. Some state laws use a slightly different name for this document, such as the "certificate" of incorporation.

Audit

The systematic (normally annual) inspection of accounting and business records involving certain standardized analyses, tests, and confirmations, which are intended to determine whether the accounting and business practices are proper. An independent audit is one conducted by an outside person or firm not connected in any way with the organization being audited. An internal audit is one that is performed by personnel of an organization to assure that internal procedures, operations, controls, and accounting practices are in proper order.

Board

Group of people elected or appointed with power to exercise certain authorities, have oversight or control of certain matters, or discharge certain functions of a fiduciary nature. This group may have certain managerial, supervisory, or investigatory functions and power in an organization or other body.

Board of Directors

The governing body of a corporation, which is authorized to act on major matters affecting the corporation. See also "Board."

Book of Discipline

Refers to *The Book of Discipline of The United Methodist Church—1996,* which is the fundamental book outlining the denomination's law, doctrine, administration, organizational work, and procedures. It is published every four years to incorporate changes adopted by the quadrennial General Conference of The United Methodist Church.

Book of Resolutions

Refers to *The Book of Resolutions of The United Methodist Church—1996,* which is a book containing all valid resolutions of the General Conference and is edited by The United Methodist Publishing House. It is published every four years to incorporate new actions taken by the quadrennial General Conference of The United Methodist Church.

Bylaws

Rules adopted by an organization for its internal governance that define the rights and obligations of various directors, officers, people, or groups within the organization and the rules for matters such as the roles of committees, calling meetings, and the like. Most state corporation laws assume that every corporation will adopt bylaws.

Closed Session

Paragraph 721 of the 1996 *Discipline* provides that, "in the spirit of openness and accountability," all United Methodist meetings shall be open. Portions of a meeting may be closed, pursuant to this disciplinary paragraph, provided that the board, committee, or other group votes to do so (by three fourths of the voting members present). Subjects that are considered appropriate for closed session are limited to "real estate matters; negotiations, when general knowledge could be harmful to the negotiation process; personnel matters; issues related to the accreditation or approval of institutions; discussions relating to litigation or collective bargaining; deployment of security personnel or devices; negotiations involving confidential third-party information; and deliberations of the Judicial Council."

Confidentiality

Something that is treated as private and not for publication or sharing with others. A confidential communication is one made under circumstances showing that the speaker intended the communication only for the ears of the person addressed.

Conflict of Interest

Term used in connection with fiduciaries and their relationship to matters of private interest or personal gain to them. Clash between the legal duty of a board member to act in the best interests of the organization and his or her own private pecuniary or personal interest. "Perception" or "appearance" of conflict of interest refers to a perceived clash between the legal duty of a board member to act in the best interests of the organization and his or her own private pecuniary or personal interest. The perception or appearance of a conflict clouds the board member's integrity in the decision-making process.

Duty of Care

Legal duty of directors and officers of an organization to act for the organization in the same manner that an ordinarily prudent person would act under similar circumstances in managing his or her own business affairs. This means that actions should be taken by board members only if they have complete information and have been reasonably diligent (such as attending meetings, reading agenda materials, asking questions, and having adequate information to make decisions).

Duty of Loyalty

Legal duty of directors and officers of an organization to act at all times in the best interests of the organization, instead of in their own best interests.

Embezzlement

The fraudulent and illegal appropriation of property by one lawfully entrusted with its possession. To wilfully take—through some office, employment, or position of trust—another's money or property for one's own use.

Fiduciary Duty

A duty to act for someone else's benefit while subordinating one's personal interests to that of the other person. It is the highest duty that the law imposes on a person to act in the interests of someone other than oneself.

Foundation

A permanent fund established and maintained by contributions for benevolent purposes. It also refers to an organization that manages such a fund.

General Council on Finance and Administration

Often referred to as GCFA, this is the general agency of The United Methodist Church charged with (among other duties) preserving and protecting the financial and legal interests of the denomination and assisting and advising jurisdictions, annual conferences, districts, and local churches on matters related to business administration, investment and property management, and auditing. The council maintains a file of legal briefs related to cases involving denominational interests. Additional information about GCFA is available at their Web site (http://www.gcfa.org).

Group Ruling

The 501(c)(3) income tax exemption granted by the Internal Revenue Service to the General Council on Finance and Administration. GCFA administers and manages the exemption for all affiliated United Methodist organizations, such as local churches.

Internal Controls

Systematic safeguards that are used to assure that an organization's financial transactions are properly authorized, appropriately executed, physically secured, and accurately recorded in accordance with the organization's policies and management's intentions. Internal controls are also mechanisms that provide a safety net for early detection and correction of actions that override or disregard the other internal-control safeguards.

Personal Liability

The liability of the officers, directors, and employees (and, at times, members) of an organization, under certain laws, by which they may be held individually responsible and liable for the actions, inactions, and debts of the organization.

Quid Pro Quo

Translated as "what for what" or "something for something" or "this for that." Used in law for the giving of one valuable thing for another.

Quorum

The number of members who must be present in a deliberative body before business may be transacted (ordinarily, a majority of the entire body, unless the organization's articles of incorporation, bylaws, or the *Discipline* otherwise provide).

Reservation of Rights

Phrase commonly used in the insurance industry when a liability insurance carrier is called upon to defend and indemnify its insured in a lawsuit and the carrier agrees to provide a defense (an attorney) but reserve all rights as to whether it is obligated under the insurance contract or law to pay for any court judgment if/when liability is determined. An insurance carrier's reservation of rights is usually spelled out in a "reservation of rights" letter sent to the insured by the carrier.

Tax Exemption

Immunity from the obligation of paying taxes in whole or in part. It may refer to an exemption from paying income taxes granted by the Internal Revenue Service for charitable, religious, and educational organizations. It also may refer to an exemption from paying property taxes granted by state and local taxing authorities. It also may refer to an exemption from paying state and/or local sales taxes granted by state and local taxing authorities. An exemption granted for income-tax purposes is not the same as an exemption granted for sales or property taxes. These types of exemptions must be separately applied for and granted by the appropriate taxing authorities.

Trust

An ongoing legal entity created by a grantor for the benefit of designated beneficiaries under the laws of the state. It also refers to the document that establishes the trust. The basic elements of a trust are a beneficiary, a trustee, some property/assets that are intended by the trust to be for the benefit of the designated beneficiaries, the delivery to the trustee of that property/assets, and the management and distribution of that property by the trustee in the best interests of the beneficiary.

Trustee

A person who holds property/assets for the benefit of another and who, for that reason, has a fiduciary duty to act in the best interests of the beneficiary. The term is sometimes used interchangeably with the term *director* on a board of directors.